Introduction The Role of Ethics in Political Narratives

With many campaigns across decades, I felt the exhilaration of winning and the pain of losing, but always kept learning. Whilst we all think we understand how campaigns work, things always change and without a good structure and planning situations can quickly unravel and messaging can be lost. Writing a short book on the politics of persuasion is my small part to help to educate others on how persuasive techniques are used in political contexts. By exploring topics such as propaganda, manipulation, and rhetoric, maybe future campaign managers and candidates can become more critical thinkers and better understand the power dynamics at play in political discourse.

Additionally, by sharing these insights I hope we can contribute to the ongoing conversation about ethics, emotions and influence in the political sphere. I am hopeful that more brilliant minds will come forward and help build the world we can all be proud of.

Contents

Included in printed version

A Examples of winning campaigns

B Your baseline campaign check list

C Space for working notes

The Politics of Persuasion: Crafting Campaign Narratives

Chapter 1: The Art of Political Persuasion

Chapter 1: The Art of Political Persuasion

Understanding Persuasion in Politics

Understanding persuasion in politics is crucial for comprehending how campaigns shape the electorate's opinions and behaviours. Political persuasion involves the strategic use of language, imagery, and emotional appeals to influence voters' perceptions and decisions. Campaigns are not merely about presenting policies; they are about crafting narratives that resonate with the values and experiences of the target audience. By understanding the mechanisms of persuasion, voters can better analyse the messages they encounter and make informed choices

At the heart of political persuasion lies the concept of framing. Framing refers to the way issues are presented and contextualized, which can significantly alter public perception. For instance, a candidate may frame an economic policy as a means of fostering growth and job creation, while opponents might frame it as a threat to social welfare. These different frames can lead to divergent interpretations and responses from the electorate. Thus, recognizing how issues are framed can empower voters to critically assess the rhetoric employed during campaigns.

Emotional appeals play a significant role in political persuasion as well. Campaigns often leverage emotions such as fear, hope, or anger to connect with voters on a deeper level. For example, a candidate might use imagery of struggling families to evoke empathy and encourage a sense of urgency about addressing economic disparities. This emotional engagement can be more impactful than rational arguments alone, as voters often make decisions based on feelings rather than facts. Understanding the emotional undercurrents of political messaging can help voters navigate the often charged atmosphere of political discourse.

In addition to framing and emotional appeals, the credibility of the messenger is a critical factor in political persuasion. Voters are more likely to be persuaded by candidates who they perceive as trustworthy and relatable. This perception can be shaped by a candidate's background, previous experiences, and public persona. Campaigns often invest significant resources in building a candidate's image to enhance their credibility. For voters, recognizing the dynamics of trust and credibility can illuminate why certain candidates resonate more than others in the political arena.

Finally, the digital landscape has transformed the way political persuasion operates. Social media platforms allow campaigns to reach and influence voters directly, bypassing traditional media gatekeepers. This direct engagement creates both opportunities and challenges for voters. While they can access a wider range of viewpoints and information, they must also navigate misinformation and biased content. Understanding the role of digital media in political persuasion equips voters to critically analyse the information they encounter and to engage thoughtfully in the political process.

Historical Context of Political Rhetoric

Political rhetoric has evolved significantly through history, shaped by cultural, social, and technological changes. In ancient Greece, rhetoric was considered an essential skill for citizens engaged in democracy. Figures like Aristotle emphasized the importance of persuasive speech in public life, believing it was vital for civic participation and the governance of society. The political oratory of figures such as Pericles exemplified how rhetoric could mobilize citizens and inspire collective action, laying the groundwork for future political discourse.

During the Roman Republic, rhetoric was further refined and institutionalized. Cicero, a prominent statesman and orator, integrated philosophical reasoning with persuasive techniques, demonstrating how rhetoric could be used not only to influence public opinion but also to uphold justice and moral integrity in governance. This period highlighted the dual role of rhetoric: as a tool for political power and as a means of ethical persuasion, emphasizing the responsibility of speakers to their audiences. The legacy of Roman rhetorical practices continued to influence political communication throughout the Middle Ages and into the Renaissance.

The advent of print technology in the 15th century marked a pivotal moment in the history of political rhetoric. The printing press enabled ideas to spread rapidly, allowing pamphlets and newspapers to reach a wider audience. This democratization of information transformed political discourse, as individuals could engage with ideas outside traditional public speaking venues. The American and French Revolutions exemplify this shift, where printed materials fueled revolutionary sentiments and mobilized the masses, demonstrating the power of rhetoric in shaping political landscapes.

The 20th century saw the rise of mass media, further altering the context of political rhetoric. Radio and television introduced new formats for persuasion, shifting the dynamics of political campaigns. Politicians like Franklin D. Roosevelt used radio effectively to connect with citizens during the Great Depression, while John F. Kennedy's televised debates showcased the importance of visual presence in political communication. This era underscored the necessity for candidates to craft narratives that resonated emotionally with voters, often employing techniques from advertising and public relations to enhance their appeal.

In the contemporary political arena, digital communication has transformed rhetoric once again. Social media platforms enable instant interaction and feedback, allowing political messages to be disseminated and contested in real time. This has led to the rise of personalized and targeted campaigning, where understanding voter demographics and preferences is crucial. The historical context of political rhetoric illustrates how adaptation to new mediums and audience expectations remains essential for effective communication in campaigns and elections, highlighting the ongoing interplay between rhetoric, technology, and political engagement.

The Role of Storytelling in Campaigns

Storytelling has emerged as a fundamental component of political campaigns, serving as a powerful tool to connect with voters on an emotional level. In an age where information is abundant yet often fleeting, compelling narratives can cut through the noise and resonate with the electorate. Campaigns that effectively utilize storytelling can humanize candidates, clarify complex issues, and create a sense of urgency that mobilizes voters. By weaving personal anecdotes and relatable experiences into their messaging, candidates can foster a deeper connection with their audience, transforming abstract policies into relatable human stories.

At the core of effective campaign storytelling is authenticity. Voters are increasingly savvy and can discern when a narrative feels contrived or overly polished. Candidates who share genuine experiences, challenges, and successes tend to build trust and credibility. This authenticity allows voters to see candidates not just as politicians but as individuals with shared values and concerns. For instance, a candidate discussing their upbringing in a struggling neighborhood can evoke empathy and understanding, making their policy proposals on education and economic reform more impactful.

Moreover, storytelling in campaigns can simplify complex political issues, making them more accessible to the average voter. Political jargon and dense policy papers can alienate constituents, but stories have the power to frame these issues in relatable terms. By illustrating the real-life implications of policies through personal narratives or testimonials, candidates can demystify their platforms. For example, a story about a family struggling with healthcare costs can highlight the need for reform in a way that statistics alone cannot. This approach not only informs voters but also encourages them to engage with the issues more deeply.

The narrative structure of a campaign also plays a crucial role in shaping the overall message and strategy. Campaigns often adopt a central theme or storyline that guides all communications, from speeches to advertisements. This cohesive narrative helps create a memorable identity for the candidate, making it easier for voters to recall their key messages. Effective use of metaphors and symbols within this narrative can also enhance its impact, as they tap into shared cultural understandings and values. A candidate who positions themselves as a "bridge-builder" may invoke imagery of unity and collaboration, appealing to voters' desires for inclusivity and progress.

Finally, storytelling in campaigns extends beyond the candidates themselves; it includes the narratives crafted by supporters, grassroots organizations, and the media. These narratives can amplify or challenge a candidate's message, demonstrating the interconnected nature of political storytelling. Social media platforms have further democratized storytelling, allowing diverse voices to share their experiences and perspectives. Campaigns that embrace this multifaceted storytelling approach can create a broader dialogue around their issues, fostering a sense of community and shared purpose among voters. As the landscape of campaigns continues to evolve, the role of storytelling will remain essential in shaping political narratives and influencing electoral outcomes.

Chapter 2: Crafting the Narrative

Chapter 2: Crafting the Narrative

Identifying Key Messages

Identifying key messages is a fundamental step in crafting effective campaign narratives. Key messages serve as the backbone of a campaign's communication strategy, ensuring that all outreach efforts are consistent and resonate with the target audience. For voting adults, campaigners, educators, and politically aware individuals, understanding how to distil complex political ideas into clear, compelling messages is crucial. This clarity not only aids in voter comprehension but also enhances engagement, allowing for more informed decision-making when it comes to elections.

To begin identifying key messages, campaigns must first understand their core values and objectives. This involves a comprehensive analysis of the political landscape, including the key issues that matter most to the electorate. Engaging in research through surveys, focus groups, and community forums can provide invaluable insights into what resonates with constituents. Such engagement not only helps in pinpointing the priorities of voters but also fosters a sense of community involvement and ownership in the political process.

Once the essential themes and priorities are established, the next step is to articulate these messages in a way that is both relatable and memorable. This requires the use of language that speaks directly to the experiences and concerns of the audience. For instance, when addressing parents, messages may focus on education reform, child welfare, or economic stability. Employing storytelling techniques can further enhance the impact of these messages, as narratives that evoke emotion can create a deeper connection with voters, making the campaign more relatable and trustworthy.

It is also essential to test these key messages to ensure their effectiveness. Campaigns can utilize various methods, such as A/B testing in advertisements or monitoring social media engagement, to gauge voter reactions. Feedback from these tests can reveal which messages resonate most, allowing campaigns to refine their approach. This iterative process ensures that the messaging remains relevant and impactful throughout the campaign, adapting to the evolving political climate and voter sentiments.

Finally, consistency in delivering key messages across all platforms is vital for building trust and credibility. Whether through speeches, social media, or traditional media channels, campaigns should maintain a unified narrative that reinforces their core values. This coherence not only strengthens the campaign's identity but also helps in establishing a lasting connection with voters. By effectively identifying and communicating key messages, campaigns can navigate the complex landscape of political theatre, ultimately persuading and mobilizing the electorate toward their vision.

Building a Cohesive Story

Building a cohesive story is essential in political campaigns, as it serves as the backbone of a candidate's narrative. A well-structured story helps voters connect emotionally with the candidate, making it easier for them to understand their vision and values. To craft a cohesive narrative, it is crucial to identify the core message that encapsulates the candidate's goals and beliefs. This message should resonate with the audience's experiences and aspirations, allowing them to envision a future that aligns with the candidate's platform.

The elements of a cohesive story include character, conflict, and resolution. The candidate often serves as the protagonist, embodying the values and experiences that voters can relate to. By sharing personal anecdotes and relatable struggles, candidates can humanize themselves and create a bond with the electorate. Furthermore, identifying the challenges facing the community or nation adds depth to the narrative. By articulating these conflicts clearly, candidates can position themselves as the solution, demonstrating how their leadership can lead to positive change.

Consistency is vital in maintaining a cohesive story throughout the campaign. Every speech, advertisement, and public appearance should reinforce the central narrative. This consistency builds trust with voters, who often scrutinize candidates for authenticity. If a candidate's message shifts erratically or is contradicted by their actions, it can lead to scepticism and disengagement from the electorate. Therefore, a well-defined storyline that echoes across all platforms helps solidify a candidate's identity in the minds of voters.

Utilizing storytelling techniques can enhance the effectiveness of a campaign narrative. Visual elements, such as compelling imagery and videos, can underscore key themes and evoke emotions. Additionally, using metaphors and analogies makes complex political issues more accessible, allowing voters to grasp the implications of policies easily. Engaging storytelling invites the electorate to participate in the narrative, fostering a sense of belonging and shared purpose, which is critical during elections.

To build a cohesive story, candidates should also be attuned to their audience's values and concerns. Conducting thorough research on the electorate can provide insights into what resonates most with voters. Tailoring the narrative to reflect the community's priorities not only reinforces the candidate's relatability but also demonstrates an understanding of the electorate's needs. By weaving voters' stories into the broader narrative, candidates can cultivate a sense of unity and collective identity, ultimately enhancing their persuasive power in the political arena.

The Importance of Authenticity

Authenticity in political communication serves as a crucial element in shaping the narratives that resonate with voters. In an age where scepticism towards politicians is prevalent, the need for candidates to present themselves as genuine and relatable is more significant than ever. Voters are increasingly discerning; they seek candidates who not only articulate their positions clearly but also demonstrate honesty and integrity. This authenticity fosters trust, a vital currency in the world of politics, as it enables candidates to connect with constituents on a personal level, making their messages more impactful.

The role of authenticity extends beyond merely presenting a polished image. It involves the congruence between a candidate's words and actions. When candidates align their policies and campaign strategies with their true beliefs and values, they create a sense of credibility that can enhance their appeal. Voters are keenly aware of inconsistencies and disingenuous behaviours, often leading to disillusionment. Therefore, candidates who embrace their authentic selves and communicate their genuine motivations are more likely to attract and retain supporters who feel a sense of alignment with those values.

Moreover, authenticity influences the emotional landscape of political campaigns. Stories of personal experiences and challenges can humanize candidates, making them more relatable to voters. In a political theatre often dominated by scripted speeches and choreographed appearances, moments of vulnerability or candidness can break through the noise. When candidates share their journeys, struggles, and successes, they create a narrative that invites voters to see them not just as politicians but as individuals with whom they can empathize. This emotional connection can significantly enhance voter engagement and loyalty.

In the context of political education, understanding the importance of authenticity is essential for both aspiring politicians and voters. Educators can play a pivotal role by encouraging critical thinking about the narratives presented during campaigns. By analysing the authenticity of candidates, students can better appreciate the complexities of political communication and the importance of integrity in leadership. This knowledge empowers voters to make informed decisions based on the authenticity of the candidates rather than the superficial allure of their campaign tactics.

Ultimately, authenticity serves as a foundational pillar in the politics of persuasion. It shapes not only how candidates are perceived but also how effectively they can engage with the electorate. In a landscape where political theatre often overshadows substantive discourse, the power of authenticity can lead to more meaningful conversations about policy and governance. As voting adults, Campaigners, educators, and politically aware individuals navigate the complexities of campaigns and elections, recognizing and valuing authenticity in political narratives will be crucial for fostering a healthier democratic process.

Chapter 3: The Influence of Media

Chapter 3: The Influence of Media

Traditional Media vs. Digital Media

The landscape of political communication has been profoundly transformed by the emergence of digital media, presenting a stark contrast to traditional media forms such as newspapers, television, and radio. Traditional media has long been regarded as the primary source of information for voters, shaping public opinion through carefully curated news stories and political coverage. This conventional framework typically involves a one-way communication model, where journalists and media outlets present information to the audience, who receive it passively. In the context of campaigns and elections, traditional media serves as a platform for candidates to convey their messages, engage in debates, and respond to current events, all while being subject to editorial oversight and journalistic standards.

In contrast, digital media has revolutionized how political narratives are crafted and disseminated. The rise of social media platforms, blogs, podcasts, and streaming services has empowered candidates and political organizations to communicate directly with voters, bypassing traditional gatekeepers. This two-way communication model facilitates real-time interaction, allowing for immediate feedback and engagement. Campaigns can now utilize targeted advertising and data analytics to reach specific demographics, tailoring messages to resonate with diverse voter groups. This shift not only amplifies the candidates' voices but also democratizes the political discourse, enabling a broader range of viewpoints to surface.

The immediacy and accessibility of digital media often lead to a more dynamic political environment, wherein stories can evolve rapidly. Information can spread virally, sometimes outpacing traditional media's ability to fact-check or contextualize it. This phenomenon can create challenges for political candidates, who must navigate the potential for misinformation and rapid public backlash. Traditional media, with its established protocols for fact-checking and editorial integrity, traditionally provides a more stable foundation for political narratives. However, the speed and reach of digital media can overshadow these practices, placing candidates in a position where they must constantly respond to emerging narratives or misrepresentations.

Moreover, the audience's engagement with traditional versus digital media differs significantly. Traditional media often engages voters through passive consumption, where individuals absorb information without direct interaction. In contrast, digital media encourages active participation, where voters can comment, share, and even create content related to political campaigns. This interactivity fosters a sense of community among politically engaged individuals but can also lead to echo chambers, where like-minded individuals reinforce each other's views without exposure to opposing perspectives. Understanding this distinction is critical for candidates and strategists as they craft their campaign narratives to appeal to an increasingly engaged and diverse electorate.

Ultimately, the interplay between traditional and digital media shapes the political landscape in profound ways. While traditional media remains a vital source of credibility and authority, digital media offers unparalleled opportunities for engagement and outreach. As campaigns evolve, the ability to blend these two forms of media becomes essential. Successful candidates will need to harness the strengths of both traditional and digital platforms to effectively communicate their messages, engage with voters, and navigate the complexities of modern political discourse. In this new era of political theatre, the art of persuasion hinges on understanding and leveraging the distinct characteristics of each medium to craft compelling campaign narratives that resonate with a politically aware audience.

The Role of Social Media in Campaign Narratives

Social media has fundamentally transformed the landscape of political communication, serving as a crucial platform for crafting and disseminating campaign narratives. In an era where information is consumed rapidly and often without the filter of traditional journalism, candidates utilize social media to bypass conventional media channels and connect directly with voters. This direct line of communication allows for the immediate sharing of messages, policies, and personal stories, which can significantly influence public perception and voter engagement. The immediacy of social media also means that narratives can be adapted in real-time in response to emerging events, ensuring that campaigns remain relevant and resonant with the electorate.

The ability of social media to foster community engagement plays a pivotal role in shaping campaign narratives. Candidates often create online spaces where supporters can gather, share experiences, and discuss issues that matter to them. These digital communities not only rally support but also generate grassroots content that can amplify the campaign's message. User-generated content, such as testimonials, endorsements, and viral posts, can carry a sense of authenticity that is often more persuasive than traditional advertisements. This phenomenon underscores the importance of cultivating an active and engaged online community, as it can significantly enhance the narrative being presented to the broader electorate.

Moreover, social media platforms enable targeted messaging based on demographic and psychographic data. Campaigns can tailor their narratives to resonate with specific voter segments, such as young voters, parents, or marginalized communities. By analysing user behaviour and preferences, political strategists can craft messages that address the unique concerns and aspirations of these groups. This targeted approach not only increases the likelihood of reaching the right audience but also fosters a sense of personal connection between candidates and voters, making the campaign narrative more impactful and memorable.

However, the role of social media in campaign narratives is not without its challenges. The rapid spread of misinformation and disinformation can distort narratives and undermine the integrity of campaigns. False information can go viral, leading to confusion and scepticism among voters. Candidates must navigate this landscape carefully, ensuring that their messages are clear, accurate, and consistent while also being prepared to counteract any misleading narratives that may emerge. This requires a proactive approach to communication, where campaigns not only promote their narratives but also defend against attacks that seek to misrepresent their positions or undermine their credibility.

Ultimately, the role of social media in shaping campaign narratives highlights the evolving nature of political discourse in the digital age. As voters increasingly rely on social media for information, candidates must harness these platforms effectively to craft compelling narratives that resonate with their audience. The interplay between narrative construction, community engagement, targeted messaging, and the challenge of misinformation creates a complex environment where the stakes are high. For voting adults, campaigners, educators, and political students, understanding this dynamic is essential for navigating the current political landscape and recognizing the power of social media in influencing electoral outcomes.

Managing Media Relations

Managing media relations is a critical component of any successful political campaign. In an era dominated by digital communication and 24-hour news cycles, understanding how to navigate the media landscape can significantly influence public perception and voter behaviour. Candidates must recognize that the media serves not only as a conduit for information but also as a powerful player in shaping narratives.

Establishing positive relationships with journalists and media outlets is essential for ensuring that campaign messages are communicated effectively and accurately.

One key strategy in managing media relations is proactive engagement. Campaigns should develop a comprehensive media strategy that outlines key messages, target audiences, and preferred communication channels. Regular press releases, media briefings, and interviews can help maintain visibility and foster goodwill with reporters. By anticipating questions and providing timely information, campaigns can position themselves as reliable sources, making it more likely that their narratives will be reported favourably. Additionally, cultivating relationships with local media can enhance grassroots support, as community outlets often have a strong influence on public opinion.

Crisis management is another vital aspect of media relations. In the fast-paced world of politics, unforeseen events and controversies can arise at any moment. Campaigns must be prepared with a crisis communication plan that addresses potential issues swiftly and transparently. This involves designating a spokesperson, crafting clear messaging, and choosing the right platforms for dissemination. A well-handled crisis can mitigate damage and even turn a negative situation into an opportunity for demonstrating accountability and responsiveness, thereby reinforcing the candidate's image in the eyes of voters.

Moreover, leveraging social media has become indispensable in managing media relations. Platforms like Twitter, Facebook, and Instagram allow campaigns to communicate directly with the electorate, bypassing traditional media filters. This direct line of communication can be used to amplify key messages, respond to misinformation, and engage with supporters in real-time. However, it is crucial to approach social media strategically, as the viral nature of content can quickly escalate situations beyond control. Campaigns should ensure that their social media presence aligns with their overall messaging and that they maintain a consistent voice across all channels.

Finally, evaluating media coverage and maintaining a feedback loop is essential for refining media relations strategies. Campaigns should monitor press coverage, assess public sentiment, and analyse the effectiveness of their communication efforts. Utilizing tools such as media tracking services can provide insights into how narratives are being crafted and perceived. By understanding which messages resonate and which do not, campaigns can adapt their strategies to better connect with voters. Continuous improvement in media relations ultimately leads to a more coherent and persuasive campaign narrative, reinforcing the candidate's positioning in the competitive political arena.

Chapter 4: Targeting the Audience

Chapter 4: Targeting the Audience

Understanding Voter Demographics

Understanding voter demographics is crucial for any political campaign aiming to craft effective narratives and strategies. Voter demographics encompass various characteristics that define the electorate, including age, gender, race, education level, and socioeconomic status. By analysing these factors, campaigns can tailor their messages and outreach efforts to resonate with specific groups, ultimately enhancing voter engagement and turnout. A comprehensive understanding of these demographics allows candidates to identify key voter blocs and the issues that matter most to them, creating a more focused and impactful campaign strategy.

One of the most significant demographic factors is age. Different generations often prioritize distinct issues based on their life experiences and current realities. For instance, younger voters may be more concerned with climate change and student debt, while older voters might prioritize healthcare and retirement security. By segmenting the electorate by age, campaigns can develop targeted messaging that speaks directly to the unique concerns of each generation. This approach not only fosters a sense of connection with voters but also increases the likelihood of mobilizing them to participate in the electoral process.

Gender and race also play pivotal roles in shaping voter demographics. Women and minority groups have historically faced different challenges and barriers that influence their political priorities and voting behaviours. An understanding of these dynamics enables campaigns to create narratives that address the specific needs and aspirations of these populations. For example, highlighting issues such as reproductive rights, racial justice, and equitable economic opportunities can resonate deeply with these voters. By acknowledging and addressing the concerns of diverse demographic groups, campaigns can build broader coalitions and foster more inclusive political discourse.

Education level is another critical demographic variable that influences voter preferences. Voters with higher education levels may prioritize issues such as innovation, technology, and educational reform, while those with lower educational attainment might be more focused on job security and economic stability. Campaigns that recognize the educational backgrounds of their target audiences can design messages that appeal to their values and experiences. Tailoring communication to reflect the concerns of different educational demographics not only enhances engagement but also reflects a candidate's understanding of the electorate's diverse needs.

Lastly, socioeconomic status significantly impacts voter behaviour and attitudes. Wealthier individuals may prioritize tax policies and business regulations, while those with lower incomes may focus on social safety nets and affordable housing. Understanding these economic divides is essential for crafting credible narratives that resonate with voters from various financial backgrounds. By addressing the economic realities faced by different demographic groups, campaigns can build trust and credibility, ultimately persuading voters to support their vision for the future. Engaging with voter demographics in a nuanced and informed manner is essential for any political campaign striving for success in today's complex electoral landscape.

Tailoring Messages for Different Groups

Tailoring messages for different groups is a fundamental aspect of political campaigning that can significantly influence the effectiveness of communication strategies. As campaigns seek to resonate with diverse audiences, understanding the unique values, concerns, and motivations of each group becomes imperative. Political theatre plays a crucial role in this process, as it provides a platform for candidates to showcase their narratives in ways that engage and persuade varied demographics. Crafting messages that are specifically tailored to the audience not only enhances relatability but also fosters a sense of connection between the candidate and constituents.

One of the primary considerations in message tailoring is demographic segmentation. Different groups, such as voting adults, parents, educators, and politically aware individuals, possess distinct priorities and concerns. For instance, parents may prioritize education and childcare policies, while politically aware individuals might focus on broader systemic issues such as campaign finance reform or climate change. By identifying these key issues relevant to each group, campaigns can construct messages that directly address their interests, making the communication more impactful and meaningful.

In addition to demographic segmentation, understanding the cultural and social contexts of each group is essential for effective messaging. Political narratives must resonate with the cultural experiences and social realities of the audience. This involves utilizing language, symbols, and references that reflect the values and beliefs of the group. For example, educators may respond positively to messages that emphasize the importance of investing in public education, whereas a message focused on economic stability might resonate more with working adults. By aligning messages with the cultural contexts of the audience, campaigns can create a deeper emotional connection that enhances persuasion.

Utilizing storytelling techniques can further enhance the tailoring of messages for different groups. Narratives that incorporate personal stories, case studies, or testimonials can illustrate the impact of policies on individuals' lives. This approach not only humanizes the message but also allows voters to see the real-world implications of political decisions. For example, sharing a story about a student overcoming obstacles due to educational reforms can effectively engage both parents and educators by highlighting shared values around success and opportunity. Through compelling storytelling, campaigns can capture attention and evoke empathy, ultimately driving voter engagement.

Lastly, feedback and adaptability are critical elements in the process of tailoring messages. Campaigns should actively seek input from their target audiences to understand how messages are received and what resonates most effectively. This feedback loop allows for adjustments and refinements to be made, ensuring that the messaging remains relevant and impactful. In the dynamic landscape of political theatre, the ability to pivot and modify narratives in response to audience reactions can be a decisive factor in a campaign's success. By prioritizing audience engagement and responsiveness, campaigns can create a more inclusive and persuasive political discourse.

Engaging Parents and Educators

Engaging parents and educators in political campaigns is essential for crafting compelling narratives that resonate with voters. These groups are not only influential within their own spheres but also serve as critical conduits of information and opinion within their communities. To effectively engage these stakeholders, campaign narratives must address their specific concerns and aspirations, thereby fostering a sense of ownership and involvement in the political process. By framing issues such as education funding, school safety, and curriculum quality in relatable terms, campaigns can create a powerful dialogue that aligns political goals with the values held by parents and educators.

One effective strategy for engaging parents is to highlight the direct impact of policies on their children's education and well-being. Campaign narratives should present clear, relatable scenarios that illustrate how proposed changes will benefit families, such as increased funding for public schools or initiatives aimed at reducing class sizes. By using real-life examples and testimonials from other parents and educators, campaigns can create an emotional connection that encourages support and advocacy. This not only empowers parents to become vocal supporters but also transforms them into active participants in the campaign narrative, amplifying its reach within their networks.

Educators, on the other hand, often seek acknowledgment of their professional expertise and the challenges they face in the classroom. Campaigns should engage educators by recognizing their insights and incorporating their feedback into policy proposals. This can be accomplished through town hall meetings, focus groups, or surveys that actively involve educators in the campaign conversation. By positioning educators as key stakeholders in the narrative, campaigns can build trust and credibility, demonstrating that they value the input of those who are on the front lines of education. This approach can lead to stronger alliances and a more robust grassroots movement.

Moreover, the integration of digital platforms is crucial for reaching both parents and educators effectively. Campaigns should utilize social media, webinars, and online forums to disseminate information and foster discussions around educational issues. Creating shareable content that resonates with the values of these groups can enhance engagement and encourage them to advocate for the campaign within their own circles. By leveraging technology, campaigns can ensure that their messages are not only heard but also actively discussed, creating a ripple effect that extends beyond traditional campaign outreach.

Ultimately, the success of political campaigns hinges on the ability to engage and mobilize parents and educators as vital allies. By crafting narratives that speak to their concerns, valuing their expertise, and utilizing modern communication tools, campaigns can create a powerful coalition that champions educational reform and broader political objectives. This engagement not only enriches the campaign narrative but also fosters a deeper connection between candidates and the communities they seek to serve, paving the way for more informed and active voter participation in the electoral process.

Chapter 5: The Role of Emotion in Politics

Chapter 5: The Role of Emotion in Politics

Emotional Appeals and Their Effectiveness

Emotional appeals are a fundamental component of political persuasion, playing a crucial role in shaping voter perceptions and decisions during campaigns. These appeals leverage the audience's feelings—such as fear, hope, anger, and empathy—to create a connection that transcends mere facts and figures. Politicians and campaign strategists understand that voters often make decisions based on how they feel rather than purely on rational analysis. This insight drives the creation of narratives that resonate emotionally, aiming to elicit responses that can significantly influence electoral outcomes.

Research shows that emotional messaging can be more effective than purely logical arguments in motivating voter turnout and engagement. For instance, fear-based appeals can highlight the potential consequences of inaction, compelling voters to support policies or candidates that promise to address their concerns. However, while fear can mobilize, it also risks alienating voters if overused or perceived as manipulative. Balancing fear with hope or empowerment can create a more compelling narrative that encourages voters to act positively rather than simply react out of fear.

Hopeful messages, on the other hand, can inspire and energize voters, particularly in challenging times. Campaigns that effectively communicate a vision for the future can foster a sense of community and shared purpose among constituents. This approach is particularly effective among demographics that may feel disenfranchised or disillusioned with the political process. By framing their policies within a hopeful narrative, candidates can cultivate a dedicated support base that feels connected to a larger movement for change.

Empathy is another powerful emotional appeal that can bridge divides and foster understanding among diverse voter groups. Campaigns that tell personal stories of individuals affected by specific policies can humanize complex political issues. By illustrating the real-life implications of political decisions, candidates can encourage voters to empathize with those impacted, prompting them to consider how their choices at the ballot box affect others in their community. This strategy not only builds emotional resonance but also encourages civic responsibility and communal solidarity.

Ultimately, the effectiveness of emotional appeals in political campaigns relies on authenticity and relatability. Voters are increasingly discerning, capable of recognizing when emotions are being manipulated for strategic gain. Campaigns that succeed in creating genuine emotional connections are often those that align their narratives with the lived experiences and values of their constituents. As the political landscape continues to evolve, the ability to craft compelling emotional narratives will remain a critical skill for candidates seeking to persuade and mobilize the electorate.

Balancing Logic and Emotion

In the realm of political persuasion, striking a balance between logic and emotion is crucial for effective campaign narratives. Voters are not only influenced by facts and figures but also by their feelings and beliefs. A campaign that relies solely on logical arguments may fail to connect with the electorate on a personal level, while one that leans too heavily on emotional appeals risks being perceived as manipulative. Therefore, successful political communication must deftly weave together rational discourse with emotional resonance to engage a diverse audience.

Logic provides the framework for understanding complex political issues, guiding voters through the maze of policies, statistics, and implications. Campaigns must present clear and coherent arguments that articulate their positions on key issues, demonstrating a thorough understanding of the political landscape. By providing well-researched data, candidates can build credibility and establish themselves as knowledgeable leaders. However, this logical foundation must be complemented by emotional storytelling that humanizes the candidate and makes the issues relatable to voters.

Emotions play a significant role in decision-making, often overriding rational thought. Campaigns that evoke feelings such as hope, fear, empathy, or anger can inspire action and drive voter engagement. For instance, personal anecdotes or testimonials from constituents can illustrate the real-world impact of policies, making them more tangible and urgent. A candidate who can effectively tap into the emotional landscape of the electorate is more likely to foster a sense of connection and loyalty, which is essential for mobilizing support.

The interplay between logic and emotion is particularly vital during critical moments in a campaign. Events such as debates or crisis situations often demand a candidate to respond swiftly and effectively. In these scenarios, a well-crafted narrative that combines factual information with emotional appeal can help candidates resonate with voters who are seeking reassurance and guidance. A balanced approach allows candidates to address concerns thoughtfully while also appealing to the hopes and fears of their audience, ultimately reinforcing their message.

To master the art of persuasion, political actors must recognize the importance of both logic and emotion in their narratives. By harnessing the strengths of each, campaigns can create a compelling and multifaceted message that captivates the electorate. This synthesis not only enhances the effectiveness of political communication but also fosters a deeper connection between candidates and voters. In an era where political theatre often overshadows substantive discourse, achieving this balance is essential for crafting narratives that not only inform but also inspire action and change.

Case Studies of Emotional Campaigns

Emotional campaigns have gained prominence in recent political landscapes, effectively harnessing the power of storytelling to resonate with voters. One notable example is Barack Obama's 2008 presidential campaign, which utilized personal narratives to create a connection with diverse voter demographics. By sharing stories of his upbringing and the struggles faced by ordinary Americans, the campaign fostered a sense of hope and unity. This approach not only highlighted policy issues but also humanized the candidate, allowing voters to see him as relatable and empathetic. The success of this emotional appeal can be attributed to its ability to forge a bond between the candidate and the electorate, ultimately influencing voter turnout and engagement.

Another case study is the 2016 campaign of Donald Trump, which employed fear and urgency as emotional drivers. Through rhetoric that emphasized threats to national security and economic stability, Trump effectively tapped into the anxieties of many voters. His use of phrases like "Make America Great Again" capitalized on nostalgia while simultaneously portraying a sense of impending crisis. This strategy, while polarizing, demonstrated how emotional narratives could mobilize a base by appealing to deep-seated fears and desires for change. The emotional resonance of Trump's campaign was evident in rally atmospheres where supporters expressed fervent loyalty, showcasing the power of fear-based narratives in political theatre.

The 2020 presidential election saw Joe Biden's campaign focus on empathy and compassion as key emotional themes. In the context of the COVID-19 pandemic and social unrest, Biden's messaging emphasized the need for healing and unity. His personal experiences with loss and resilience resonated with voters grappling with their own hardships during a tumultuous time. This narrative of empathy not only differentiated him from his opponent but also appealed to a collective desire for stability and leadership. The effectiveness of this emotional strategy was reflected in Biden's ability to garner support across traditional party lines, illustrating how a compassionate campaign can transcend divisive politics.

In local elections, emotional campaigns often manifest through personal stories that highlight community issues. For instance, a candidate running for mayor might share their own experiences growing up in the neighbourhood, discussing specific challenges faced by residents. By framing their platform around these relatable narratives, candidates can establish a sense of trust and authenticity. This grassroots approach empowers voters to see the candidates as their representatives rather than distant politicians, fostering a deeper connection that can significantly influence election outcomes. The impact of localized emotional appeals underscores the importance of understanding community values and concerns in political campaigning.

The analysis of these emotional campaigns reveals critical insights into the dynamics of political persuasion. Campaigns that effectively utilize emotional narratives tend to create stronger connections with voters, whether through hope, fear, or empathy. As political theatre continues to evolve, understanding the mechanics of emotional storytelling will be essential for future candidates. By recognizing the power of these narratives, political actors can better navigate the complexities of voter sentiment and engagement, ultimately shaping the political landscape in more profound ways.

Chapter 6: The Mechanics of Campaigning

Chapter 6: The Mechanics of Campaigning

Developing a Campaign Strategy

Developing a campaign strategy is a crucial step in ensuring the success of any political endeavour. It involves a systematic approach to defining the goals, identifying the target audience, and crafting messages that resonate with voters. A well-structured campaign strategy not only outlines the tactical aspects of the campaign but also shapes the narrative that will be communicated throughout the electoral process. It is essential for candidates to create a clear roadmap that guides their actions and decisions while engaging effectively with the electorate.

The first element of a successful campaign strategy is understanding the political landscape. This involves conducting thorough research on the demographics, values, and issues that matter most to the voters in the constituency. By analysing polling data, past election results, and social trends, candidates can gain insights into the priorities and concerns of their potential supporters. This foundational knowledge allows campaigns to tailor their messages and outreach efforts to address the specific needs and expectations of the electorate.

Next, establishing a compelling narrative is imperative. The narrative serves as the backbone of the campaign, encapsulating the candidate's vision, values, and policy proposals. A well-crafted narrative not only articulates what the candidate stands for but also connects emotionally with voters. It should be authentic and relatable, allowing voters to see the candidate as a genuine representative of their interests. By weaving personal stories and relevant experiences into the campaign narrative, candidates can foster a sense of trust and relatability, which are essential for building a strong connection with the electorate.

In addition to narrative development, setting clear objectives and measurable goals is a fundamental part of the campaign strategy. Candidates must define what success looks like, whether it's winning a specific percentage of the vote, mobilizing a certain number of volunteers, or raising a predetermined amount of funds. These goals should be realistic and aligned with the overall mission of the campaign. Regularly assessing progress against these benchmarks allows for strategic adjustments and ensures that the campaign remains focused and agile in response to changing circumstances.

Finally, an effective campaign strategy must incorporate a comprehensive outreach plan that utilizes various communication channels. This includes traditional media, social media, community engagement, and grassroots mobilization efforts. Each channel serves a unique purpose and reaches different segments of the electorate. A multi-faceted approach ensures that the campaign message is disseminated widely and consistently, maximizing impact. By actively engaging with voters through town hall meetings, online forums, and door-to-door canvassing, candidates can foster dialogue, address concerns, and solidify their presence in the community, ultimately enhancing their chances of electoral success.

The Importance of Grassroots Mobilization

Grassroots mobilization plays a crucial role in shaping the political landscape, particularly in campaigns and elections. It embodies the collective effort of individuals coming together to advocate for a cause or candidate at the local level. This form of engagement is vital in creating a sense of community and ownership among constituents, allowing them to feel that their voices matter in the larger political discourse. Unlike top-down approaches that may prioritize elite interests, grassroots movements empower ordinary citizens to influence decision-making processes and contribute to the democratic fabric of society.

One of the primary advantages of grassroots mobilization is its ability to generate authentic narratives that resonate with a diverse electorate. Campaigns that originate from the community are often more relatable and can reflect the real-life experiences of voters. This authenticity is critical in an era where scepticism towards traditional political messaging runs high. By tapping into local stories and addressing specific community needs, grassroots campaigns can craft narratives that not only engage but also inspire action among voters, fostering a sense of shared purpose that is essential for electoral success.

Moreover, grassroots mobilization enhances voter turnout, which is a vital component of any election strategy. When individuals feel directly involved in the political process, they are more likely to participate in elections. Organizers at the grassroots level engage in door-to-door canvassing, phone banking, and community events that not only raise awareness but also build relationships among voters. These personal connections can significantly impact voter enthusiasm and commitment, making grassroots efforts a powerful tool for increasing participation, especially in historically underrepresented communities.

In addition to boosting voter turnout, grassroots mobilization can influence the broader political agenda. When issues are propelled by local activists, they can gain traction and force candidates and elected officials to address them. This can lead to shifts in policy priorities, as grassroots movements often highlight concerns like education, healthcare, and social justice that may be overlooked by mainstream political narratives. As a result, grassroots organizations can serve as a check on political leaders, ensuring that they remain accountable to the needs of their constituents.

Finally, the significance of grassroots mobilization extends beyond the immediate electoral context. It fosters a culture of civic engagement that can lead to sustained political involvement among citizens. When individuals participate in grassroots campaigns, they gain valuable skills and knowledge about the political process, encouraging them to remain active in their communities long after the election is over. This ongoing engagement is essential for nurturing informed and active citizens who can advocate for their interests and contribute to a vibrant democratic society. In essence, grassroots mobilization is not just a campaign strategy; it is a foundational element for a healthy, participatory democracy.

Fundraising and Resource Allocation

Fundraising and resource allocation are critical components of any political campaign, influencing not only the viability of candidates but also the narratives they craft. In a political landscape where financial resources can dictate the extent of outreach and messaging, understanding the intricacies of fundraising becomes essential for candidates and their teams. This process often begins with establishing a compelling narrative that resonates with potential donors, allowing campaigns to tap into both small and large contributions. Engaging storytelling can evoke emotions and align the candidate's values with those of potential supporters, creating a foundation for financial backing.

Effective fundraising strategies are multifaceted, ranging from grassroots efforts to high-profile fundraising events. Grassroots campaigns rely heavily on small donations from a large base of supporters, leveraging social media and community engagement to build momentum. These approaches can foster a sense of ownership and investment among voters, as they feel directly involved in the campaign's success. On the other hand, high-dollar fundraising events often draw influential donors who can provide substantial contributions, but they come with their own set of challenges. Balancing these two approaches requires a nuanced understanding of the donor landscape and the political theatre in which candidates operate.

Resource allocation involves determining how to effectively distribute the financial contributions received to maximize campaign impact. This requires strategic planning and prioritization of campaign activities, such as advertising, outreach, and events. Campaign managers must assess which areas will yield the highest return on investment, often guided by polling data and feedback from constituents. Allocating resources effectively means not only investing in traditional media but also embracing digital platforms where voters increasingly consume information. The ability to pivot resources in response to shifting dynamics can significantly affect a campaign's trajectory.

Moreover, transparency in fundraising and resource allocation is increasingly important in today's political environment. Voters demand clarity about where campaign funds are coming from and how they are being used. Candidates who prioritize transparency can build trust with their constituents, enhancing their credibility. This can be achieved through regular updates and detailed reports on fundraising efforts and expenditures. A campaign that is open about its financial dealings can mitigate potential backlash and strengthen its narrative around integrity and accountability.

Ultimately, the interplay between fundraising and resource allocation shapes the overall narrative of a political campaign. Candidates who master this aspect of campaigning not only secure the necessary funds but also craft compelling stories that resonate with voters. As they navigate the complexities of financial support, they must remain mindful of how their funding sources and spending decisions impact public perception. Building and maintaining a strong narrative while managing resources effectively can distinguish successful campaigns in the competitive arena of politics.

Chapter 7: The Impact of Debates and Public Speaking

Chapter 7: The Impact of Debates and Public Speaking

Preparing for Public Engagements

Preparing for public engagements is a crucial step in the art of persuasion, particularly within the context of political campaigns and elections. Understanding the audience's needs and expectations can significantly enhance the effectiveness of a campaign message. Engaging with voters requires a clear strategy that goes beyond mere rhetoric. It involves a deep comprehension of the community's values, concerns, and aspirations, which can be achieved through thorough research and analysis. This groundwork lays the foundation for a compelling narrative that resonates with the audience.

One of the first steps in preparing for public engagements is defining the key messages that will be communicated. These messages should align with the overarching goals of the campaign while addressing specific issues that matter to constituents. Crafting these messages involves simplifying complex ideas into relatable concepts that can easily be understood. Political candidates must ensure that their narratives are not only informative but also emotionally appealing, as voters often make decisions based on feelings as much as facts. This emotional connection can be established through storytelling, which allows candidates to share their personal experiences and visions for the future.

Rehearsing for public engagements is equally important, as it helps candidates refine their delivery and build confidence. This practice should involve not just memorizing speeches but also engaging in mock interactions with potential voters. Role-playing different scenarios can prepare candidates for varying audience reactions and questions. It also provides an opportunity to incorporate feedback from advisors or focus groups, ensuring that the candidate's approach remains authentic and relatable. This preparation helps mitigate anxiety and allows candidates to focus on connecting with their audience during real engagements.

Additionally, understanding the logistics of public engagements is essential for a successful campaign. This includes selecting appropriate venues, timing, and formats for events, whether they are town halls, debates, or meet-and-greets. Each format presents unique challenges and opportunities for interaction. Candidates should also be prepared for the technical aspects, such as sound systems and visual aids, which can enhance the overall presentation. A well-organized event not only reflects professionalism but also creates a welcoming atmosphere for participants, encouraging open dialogue and engagement.

Finally, post-engagement reflection is a crucial component of the preparation process. Candidates should analyse what worked well and what didn't, using insights gained from voter interactions to refine their strategy moving forward. This includes gathering feedback from attendees, assessing audience reactions, and evaluating the effectiveness of the messages delivered. Continuous improvement is vital in political campaigns, as voters' opinions and concerns evolve over time. By committing to ongoing assessment and adaptation, candidates can remain responsive to their constituents and strengthen their persuasive efforts throughout the campaign.

Crafting Effective Debate Strategies

Effective debate strategies are crucial for candidates seeking to persuade voters in a highly competitive political landscape. A well-crafted debate strategy not only highlights a candidate's strengths but also addresses their opponent's weaknesses. To achieve this, candidates must first understand their audience. This involves analysing the demographic, cultural, and social factors that influence voter perceptions and preferences. By framing their arguments in a way that resonates with the electorate, candidates can create a connection that enhances their persuasiveness during debates.

One essential component of a successful debate strategy is the development of clear, concise messaging. Candidates should focus on key issues that matter to their audience, articulating their position in a way that is easy to understand. This requires candidates to distil complex policy issues into relatable narratives. Using anecdotes, statistics, and vivid imagery can help make their points more compelling. Additionally, candidates should anticipate potential counterarguments and prepare well-crafted responses to disarm critics while reinforcing their own positions.

The role of body language and delivery in debates cannot be overstated. Non-verbal communication plays a significant part in how messages are received. Candidates should practice maintaining appropriate eye contact, using gestures that emphasize their points, and managing their tone to convey confidence and sincerity. Effective debaters also know when to pause for emphasis, allowing their key messages to resonate with the audience. The combination of strong verbal and non-verbal cues can significantly enhance a candidate's persuasive power.

Debate preparation should also include researching opponents thoroughly. Understanding an opponent's positions, past statements, and voting records allows candidates to formulate effective rebuttals and expose inconsistencies. This preparation should extend beyond mere facts; it involves analysing the opponent's debate style and identifying potential weaknesses that can be exploited during the debate. By being well-informed, candidates can engage in more dynamic exchanges, which not only highlight their own strengths but also cast doubt on their opponent's credibility.

Finally, candidates must be adaptable during the debate. While having a strategy is essential, the ability to pivot in response to unexpected questions or challenges can set a candidate apart. Active listening is vital; candidates should pay close attention to their opponents and the audience's reactions, allowing them to adjust their approach in real-time. This flexibility can lead to more authentic interactions and can help candidates appear more relatable and responsive to voter concerns. In the ever-evolving arena of political theatre, being able to craft and execute effective debate strategies is essential for securing voter support.

Analysing Successful Speeches

Analysing successful speeches provides valuable insights into the art of persuasion in political campaigns. Effective speeches resonate with audiences by addressing their emotions, values, and concerns. Politicians who master this craft understand the importance of storytelling, using personal anecdotes and relatable experiences to build connections with voters. By examining the techniques employed in memorable speeches, we can glean lessons on how to communicate effectively in the political arena.

One key element of successful speeches is the use of rhetorical devices. Figures of speech such as metaphors, alliteration, and parallelism can enhance the message and make it more memorable. For instance, when politicians articulate complex ideas through simple yet powerful language, they create a sense of clarity that can galvanize support. This approach not only helps convey the message but also ensures that it sticks in the minds of the audience long after the speech ends.

Another critical aspect of effective speeches is the strategic use of emotional appeals. Politicians often tap into the emotional landscape of their audience to inspire action and foster engagement. By highlighting shared values and experiences, they can evoke feelings of hope, fear, or nostalgia, which can significantly influence voter behaviour.

Analysing speeches from historical figures reveals how emotional resonance can be a powerful tool in shaping public opinion and mobilizing support.

Furthermore, the context in which a speech is delivered plays a significant role in its effectiveness. Understanding the political climate, current events, and societal issues can help speakers tailor their messages to resonate with the audience's immediate concerns. Successful speeches often reflect a keen awareness of the audience's needs, allowing politicians to position themselves as empathetic leaders who genuinely understand the challenges faced by their constituents. This connection can enhance the credibility of the speaker and strengthen their persuasive impact.

Finally, the delivery of a speech—encompassing voice modulation, body language, and pacing—affects how the message is received. A confident and passionate delivery can amplify the message's effectiveness, capturing the audience's attention and reinforcing the speaker's credibility. By analysing the techniques used by successful speakers, aspiring politicians and communicators can learn how to refine their delivery, ultimately enhancing their ability to persuade and connect with voters in a meaningful way.

Chapter 8: Ethical Considerations in Political Persuasion

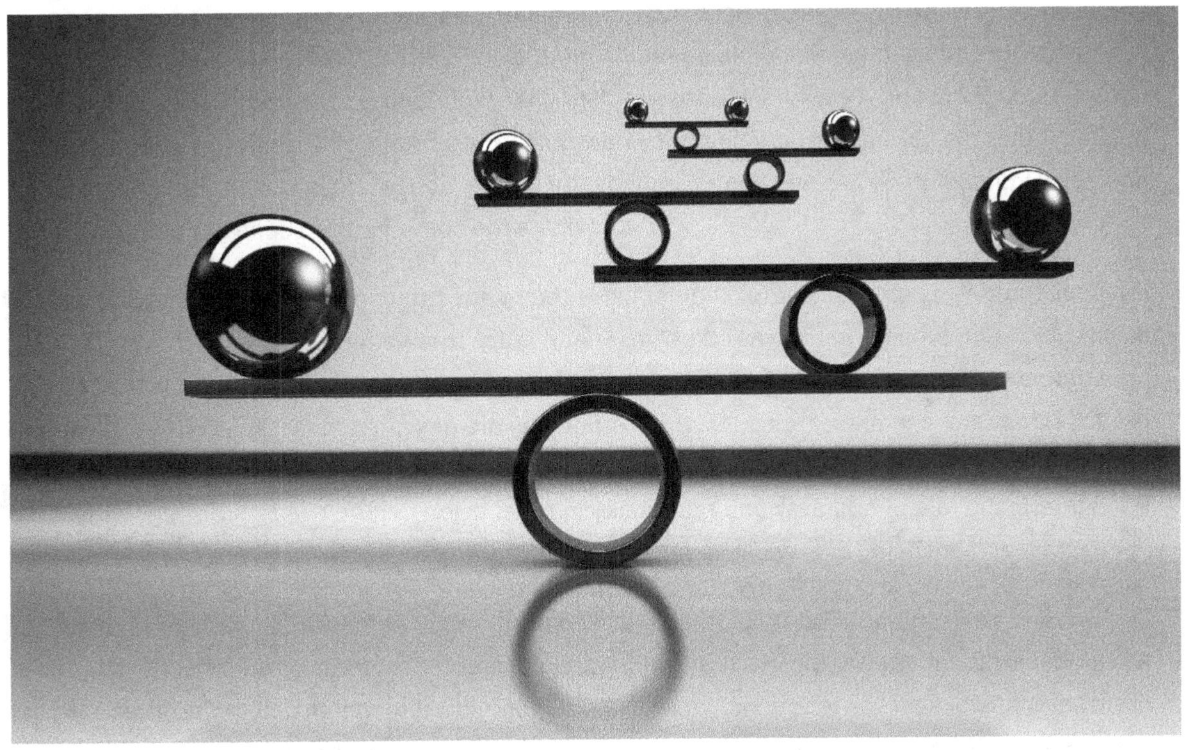

Chapter 8: Ethical Considerations in Political Persuasion

The Fine Line Between Persuasion and Manipulation

The distinction between persuasion and manipulation is crucial in the realm of political campaigns and narratives. Persuasion is often viewed as a legitimate means of influencing beliefs and behaviours through logical reasoning, ethical arguments, and emotional appeals. It aims to engage voters by presenting them with information that allows them to make informed decisions. In contrast, manipulation involves deceptive tactics that exploit emotions and biases to achieve a desired outcome, often disregarding the individual's autonomy and ability to make rational choices. Understanding this fine line is essential for voters, educators, and political students who navigate the complex landscape of political theatre.

Political campaigns routinely employ persuasive techniques to connect with voters. Candidates often craft compelling narratives that resonate with the values and aspirations of their constituents. This can include highlighting shared experiences, addressing community needs, or proposing solutions to pressing issues. Such strategies are designed to foster a sense of trust and rapport, ultimately empowering voters to support a candidate or policy based on informed choices. Recognizing the role of empathy and relatability in persuasion can help voters discern when they are being engaged in a meaningful dialogue versus when they are being led astray.

Conversely, manipulation often surfaces in the form of disinformation, fear-mongering, or emotional exploitation. Campaigns may deliberately misrepresent facts or utilize sensationalized rhetoric to provoke strong reactions, steering public opinion through anxiety rather than rational deliberation. This approach undermines the democratic process, as it can create divisions based on misinformation rather than fostering informed debate. For parents and educators, understanding these tactics is vital for guiding young voters and helping them develop critical thinking skills necessary to discern between persuasive communication and manipulative strategies.

The consequences of crossing the line from persuasion to manipulation can be profound. When political discourse devolves into manipulation, it can erode trust in institutions and lead to voter apathy or cynicism. When individuals feel they have been misled or coerced, their willingness to engage in the political process diminishes. This not only impacts individual voters but can also have a ripple effect on the overall health of democracy. Educators and political mentors play a critical role in equipping future voters with the tools to recognize these tactics, fostering a more informed electorate.

Ultimately, the challenge lies in navigating the thin boundary between persuasion and manipulation in political communication. Voters must cultivate an awareness of the methods used to influence their decisions and develop a critical lens through which to evaluate campaign messages. By fostering an understanding of ethical persuasion, stakeholders can empower individuals to engage thoughtfully with political narratives, ensuring that their choices reflect genuine beliefs and informed perspectives rather than manipulated emotions. This awareness is essential for nurturing a democracy that thrives on informed citizenry and robust political discourse.

Transparency and Accountability in Campaigns

Transparency and accountability in political campaigns are crucial elements that shape the integrity of the electoral process. In an era where misinformation can spread rapidly, voters need to trust the information presented to them by candidates and their campaigns. Transparency involves the clear communication of policies, funding sources, and the motivations behind campaign decisions, allowing voters to make informed choices. Accountability, on the other hand, focuses on holding candidates responsible for their statements and actions throughout the campaign. Together, these principles help cultivate a political environment where candidates are compelled to engage honestly with the electorate.

The significance of transparency is underscored by the increasing demand for disclosure of campaign financing. Voters are entitled to know who funding campaigns is and how that money influences political agendas. When candidates openly share their funding sources, they not only foster trust but also deter potential corruption. Campaign finance laws and regulations exist to promote this transparency, yet enforcement can be inconsistent. Therefore, it is essential for voters to remain vigilant and advocate for stricter compliance and better reporting practices. An informed electorate can challenge the status quo and demand accountability from candidates regarding their financial backers.

Accountability in campaigns also extends to the promises made by candidates. When candidates articulate their visions and propose specific policies, they should be prepared to follow through on those commitments if elected. Voter engagement does not end at the ballot box; it continues throughout the candidate's tenure in office. Organizations such as independent fact-checkers and watchdog groups play a vital role in monitoring campaign promises and evaluating the actions of elected officials. By holding candidates accountable for their words, voters can ensure that the political narrative remains rooted in reality rather than mere rhetoric.

Moreover, effective communication strategies in campaigns must prioritize transparency and accountability. Candidates who foster open dialogues with their constituents are more likely to build genuine connections and earn trust. Utilizing various platforms, including social media, town hall meetings, and public forums, allows candidates to engage with voters directly, answer questions candidly, and address concerns transparently. This approach not only enhances the candidate's credibility but also empowers voters, making them feel integral to the political process.

In conclusion, transparency and accountability are indispensable to the health of democratic campaigns. By demanding clear communication about campaign financing and holding candidates responsible for their promises, voters play a crucial role in the political theatre of campaigns and elections. As politically aware individuals, it is imperative to advocate for these values, ensuring that the narratives crafted during campaigns are both persuasive and truthful. A commitment to these principles not only enriches the electoral experience but also strengthens the foundation of democracy itself.

The Role of Ethics in Political Narratives

Ethics play a crucial role in shaping political narratives, influencing not only the perceptions of candidates but also the decisions of voters. Political narratives are crafted stories that candidates and parties use to frame their identities, policies, and visions for the future. When these narratives are underpinned by ethical considerations, they foster trust and credibility among the electorate. Conversely, when ethical standards are compromised, the resulting narratives can lead to misinformation and polarization, ultimately undermining the democratic process.

A central aspect of ethical political narratives is honesty. Candidates who prioritize transparency in their messaging are more likely to build lasting connections with voters. By providing clear, factual information about their positions and policies, they can create a narrative that resonates with the public's values and concerns. This not only enhances the legitimacy of their campaign but also encourages informed decision-making among voters. In contrast, narratives built on deception or exaggeration can yield short-term gains but often result in long-term consequences, including voter apathy and distrust in political institutions.

Furthermore, ethical considerations in political narratives extend to the representation of diverse voices and perspectives. In an increasingly multicultural society, it is vital for political narratives to reflect the experiences and needs of various demographic groups. When campaigns engage with and incorporate these perspectives, they not only enrich their narratives but also demonstrate a commitment to inclusivity and social justice. This ethical approach can enhance voter engagement, as individuals are more likely to feel represented and valued within the political discourse.

The impact of ethics in political narratives is also evident in the framing of issues and policies. Ethical storytelling requires a careful balance between advocacy and factual representation. Campaigns must navigate complex social issues without oversimplifying or sensationalizing them. Ethical narratives should promote understanding and encourage dialogue rather than division. By addressing contentious issues with integrity, candidates can elevate the quality of political discourse and foster a more informed electorate.

In conclusion, the role of ethics in political narratives is fundamental to the integrity of the electoral process. Ethical narratives not only strengthen the bond between candidates and voters but also contribute to a healthier democratic environment. As voting adults, parents, educators, and politically aware individuals engage with these narratives, they must critically assess the ethical dimensions of the messages being presented. By doing so, they can help ensure that the political theatre of campaigns and elections remains a space for genuine dialogue and responsible representation.

Chapter 9: Case Studies of Successful Campaigns

Chapter 9: Case Studies of Successful Campaigns

Analysing Notable Campaigns in History

Analysing notable campaigns in history provides valuable insights into the art of persuasion and the impact of narrative on electoral success. One of the most significant examples is Franklin D. Roosevelt's 1932 presidential campaign. In the midst of the Great Depression, Roosevelt employed a narrative that emphasized hope and recovery. His message resonated with a populace grappling with economic despair. The effective use of radio through his "fireside chats" allowed him to communicate directly with voters, fostering a personal connection that was pivotal in reshaping public perception and garnering support.

Another landmark campaign was John F. Kennedy's 1960 bid for the presidency. Kennedy's youthful image and charisma contrasted sharply with the older Richard Nixon. The first-ever televised presidential debates played a crucial role in shaping public opinion. Kennedy's mastery of media and message crafted a narrative of a new generation ready to tackle the challenges of the Cold War era. His campaign used visuals and sound bites effectively, appealing to the emotions of voters and creating a sense of urgency that propelled him to victory.

The 2008 Obama campaign also stands out as a masterclass in modern political narrative. Barack Obama's message of "Hope and Change" tapped into the public's desire for transformation after years of political disillusionment. The campaign utilized social media and grassroots mobilization to engage younger voters, fundamentally changing the landscape of political campaigning. By telling a compelling personal story interwoven with broader themes of progress and unity, Obama was able to create a powerful narrative that resonated across demographic lines, leading to an unprecedented voter turnout.

In contrast, the 2016 campaign of Donald Trump showcased a different approach to political narrative. Trump's use of populist rhetoric and a confrontational style appealed to disenchanted voters seeking an outsider perspective. His campaign effectively leveraged social media to bypass traditional media gatekeepers, allowing him to frame issues on his terms. The narrative of "Make America Great Again" tapped into feelings of nostalgia and insecurity, resonating with those who felt left behind by globalization and technological change. This campaign illustrated how narrative can be wielded to mobilize a passionate base, regardless of conventional political norms.

Finally, the analysis of these campaigns underscores the importance of adaptability in political narrative. As societal values and technology evolve, so too must the strategies employed by candidates. The ability to craft a narrative that not only speaks to current issues but also connects with the lived experiences of voters is crucial. Campaigns that succeed in this regard not only gain electoral victories but also influence the broader political discourse, setting the stage for future generations of political engagement. Understanding these historical campaigns allows voters and political students alike to recognize the significance of narrative in shaping political landscapes.

Lessons Learned from Failed Campaigns

Failed political campaigns often provide a wealth of insights that can be invaluable for future endeavours. One of the primary lessons learned is the importance of understanding the electorate. Many campaigns falter because they fail to accurately gauge the interests, values, and concerns of the voters they seek to persuade. A disconnect between a candidate's message and the electorate's needs can lead to significant missteps. Campaigns that prioritize data-driven approaches and engage in active listening are more likely to resonate with voters and avoid the pitfalls that lead to failure.

Another critical lesson from unsuccessful campaigns is the significance of a cohesive narrative. Campaigns that lack a clear and compelling story often struggle to connect with audiences. A disjointed message can confuse voters and dilute a candidate's brand. Successful campaigns learn to craft a consistent narrative that aligns with their values and objectives while being adaptable enough to address emerging issues. By creating a strong, relatable storyline, candidates can foster a sense of trust and engagement among voters, ultimately enhancing their chances of success.

The role of strategy in campaign execution cannot be overstated. Many failed campaigns demonstrate the consequences of poor strategic planning. Whether it's allocating resources ineffectively or neglecting key demographics, a lack of strategic foresight can hinder a campaign's ability to gain traction. Campaigns that assess their strengths, weaknesses, opportunities, and threats are better equipped to devise a strategy that positions them favorably in the political landscape. Learning from the miscalculations of others can help future candidates to develop more effective approaches to campaigning.

Additionally, failed campaigns often highlight the dangers of over-reliance on media and technology without authentic engagement. While digital platforms are crucial for modern campaigning, they cannot replace the value of direct voter interaction. Candidates who neglect face-to-face communication risk alienating potential supporters. Engaging with voters through town halls, community events, and personal outreach builds rapport and trust. Successful campaigns recognize the balance between using technology for outreach and maintaining genuine connections with the electorate.

Finally, analysing the aftermath of failed campaigns can reveal the importance of adaptability and resilience. The political landscape is dynamic, and campaigns must be prepared to pivot in response to changing circumstances. Learning from mistakes and being willing to adjust tactics and messaging in real time can make a significant difference in a campaign's trajectory. Those who study the failures of others understand that setbacks can serve as stepping stones to success, provided there is a commitment to learning and growth. Embracing this mindset can empower future candidates to navigate the complexities of political campaigning more effectively.

The Evolution of Campaign Strategies

The evolution of campaign strategies has been significantly influenced by changes in technology, societal values, and the political landscape itself. In the early years of American democracy, campaigns were characterized by face-to-face interactions, town hall meetings, and printed pamphlets. Candidates relied heavily on personal charisma and direct engagement with voters. This grassroots approach allowed candidates to connect with their constituents on a personal level, fostering strong relationships that were crucial for gaining support. However, as the political environment began to shift, so too did the methods by which candidates sought to persuade the electorate.

With the advent of mass media in the 20th century, campaign strategies underwent a dramatic transformation. Radio and television became essential tools for reaching a broader audience, allowing candidates to broadcast their messages far beyond local communities. This shift marked the beginning of a more sophisticated approach to campaigning, where image and presentation gained prominence. Campaign teams began to hire public relations experts and media consultants to craft messages that resonated with diverse voter demographics. The focus shifted from personal interactions to a reliance on carefully constructed narratives designed to capture public attention and sway opinions.

In the digital age, the evolution of campaign strategies took another significant leap forward. The rise of the internet and social media platforms introduced new channels for political communication, enabling campaigns to engage with voters in real-time. Social media allowed for targeted messaging, where candidates could tailor their outreach based on data analytics and voter preferences. This shift not only made campaigns more interactive but also encouraged a culture of rapid response, where candidates had to adapt their strategies on the fly to address emerging issues and criticisms. The ability to reach voters instantly transformed the political landscape, making it imperative for campaigns to be agile and responsive.

Moreover, the globalization of information has had a profound impact on how campaign narratives are shaped and disseminated. Voters are now exposed to a multitude of perspectives and influences from around the world, leading to a more informed and, at times, polarized electorate. Campaigns have had to navigate this complex environment by crafting narratives that resonate across diverse cultural contexts while being mindful of the potential for backlash. The challenge lies in striking a balance between appealing to core supporters and reaching out to undecided voters, all while maintaining a consistent message that reflects the candidate's values and vision.

As we look to the future, the evolution of campaign strategies will likely continue to adapt to technological advancements and changing voter expectations. The integration of artificial intelligence and data-driven decision-making is poised to further refine how campaigns target and engage with voters. Additionally, as issues such as climate change, social justice, and economic inequality rise to prominence, candidates will need to develop narratives that address these concerns authentically. Ultimately, the evolution of campaign strategies will remain a dynamic interplay of persuasion, innovation, and the enduring human desire for connection in the political arena.

Chapter 10: The Future of Political Narratives

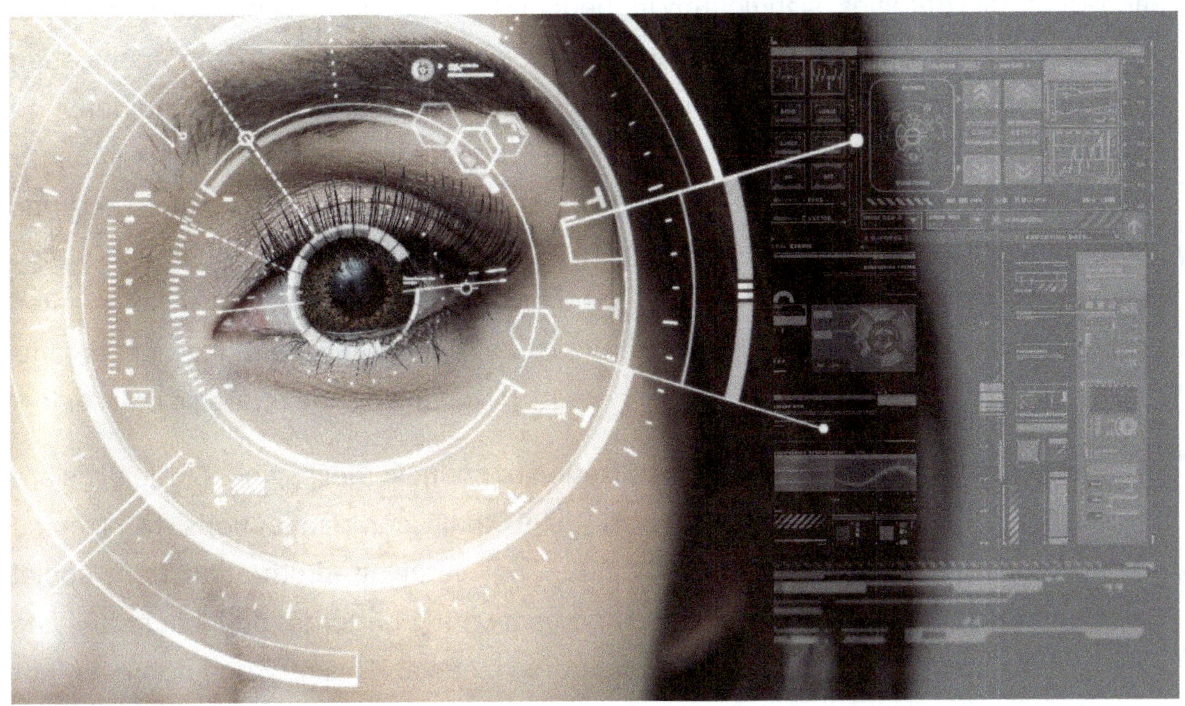

Chapter 10: The Future of Political Narratives

Emerging Trends in Political Communication

Emerging trends in political communication are reshaping the landscape of campaigns and electoral strategies, significantly influencing how candidates connect with voters. One prominent trend is the increasing reliance on digital platforms for communication and engagement. Social media has become a powerful tool for candidates to disseminate their messages, interact with constituents, and mobilize support. Platforms such as Twitter, Facebook, and Instagram allow for real-time communication, enabling campaigns to respond quickly to news events and public sentiment. This immediacy not only enhances engagement but also creates challenges, as misinformation can spread just as rapidly, necessitating vigilant fact-checking and strategic messaging.

Another significant trend is the personalization of political messaging. Campaigns are increasingly utilizing data analytics to tailor their communications to specific demographic groups and individual voters. By leveraging information from social media interactions, online behaviours, and past voting patterns, political strategists are crafting messages that resonate on a personal level. This targeted approach not only increases the likelihood of voter engagement but also raises ethical concerns regarding privacy and the manipulation of voter behaviour. As campaigns continue to refine their use of data, the line between personalized outreach and invasion of privacy becomes increasingly blurred.

The role of visual storytelling in political communication is also gaining prominence. Campaigns are increasingly employing video content as a primary means of conveying messages, driven by the understanding that visual media is more engaging and shareable than text-based content. From short clips that highlight key policy points to emotionally charged narratives that humanize candidates, video storytelling can evoke powerful emotional responses, making it a crucial element of modern political communication. This trend underscores the importance of production quality and authenticity, as voters are becoming more discerning about the content they consume and its source.

Another emerging trend is the rise of grassroots movements and citizen journalism. As traditional media outlets face declining trust and influence, individuals are taking to social media to share their perspectives and experiences related to political issues.

This shift has empowered ordinary citizens to participate in the political discourse, often leading to viral movements that can significantly impact campaigns. The democratization of information dissemination means that candidates must not only manage their own narratives but also navigate a landscape where public opinion can be shaped by voices outside of established media channels.

Lastly, the intersection of political communication and activism is becoming more pronounced, especially among younger voters. Social movements such as Black Lives Matter and climate change activism have harnessed the power of political communication to advocate for change and mobilize support. These movements often utilize social media to amplify their messages, engage supporters, and hold political figures accountable. As this trend continues, candidates will need to align their platforms with the values and concerns of these activist groups to appeal to a new generation of voters who prioritize authenticity and social justice in their political choices. This evolving dynamic indicates that the future of political communication will be characterized by a blend of traditional campaign strategies and grassroots activism.

The Role of Technology in Shaping Narratives

The role of technology in shaping narratives within the political landscape has become increasingly significant, particularly in the context of campaigns and elections. As technology evolves, it provides new platforms and tools that influence how political messages are crafted, disseminated, and received. This has led to a transformation in the way candidates communicate with voters, ultimately affecting the outcomes of elections. The use of social media, data analytics, and digital advertising has become integral to campaign strategies, allowing for targeted messaging that resonates with specific demographics.

Social media platforms have revolutionized the way candidates engage with the electorate. Through channels such as Twitter, Facebook, and Instagram, politicians can share their messages in real time, bypassing traditional media gatekeepers. This direct line of communication allows for immediate feedback and interaction with constituents, fostering a sense of connection that was previously unattainable. However, this immediacy also raises concerns about the spread of misinformation, as false narratives can quickly gain traction and influence public perception. The challenge lies in leveraging these platforms effectively while maintaining the integrity of the information being shared.

Data analytics plays a crucial role in shaping narratives by enabling campaigns to understand voter behaviour and preferences on a granular level. By analysing vast amounts of data, campaigns can identify trends, target specific voter segments, and tailor their messages accordingly. This targeted approach not only enhances the effectiveness of the narrative but also increases the likelihood of engagement from voters. The ability to predict and influence voter behaviour through data-driven strategies has become a cornerstone of modern political campaigning, highlighting the importance of technology in narrative formation.

Digital advertising further amplifies the reach of campaign narratives, allowing for strategic placement of messages across various online platforms. Campaigns can utilize sophisticated algorithms to ensure that their advertisements are seen by the most relevant audiences, maximizing the impact of their messaging. This targeted advertising not only increases visibility but also allows for the testing of different narratives to see which resonates most with voters. As a result, the narratives that emerge during campaigns are often a reflection of the data-driven insights gained through technology, showcasing the interplay between innovation and political storytelling.

Ultimately, the integration of technology in shaping political narratives raises important questions about authenticity, trust, and the future of democratic discourse. As campaigns increasingly rely on technology to craft their messages, the challenge remains to strike a balance between effective communication and the ethical responsibilities that come with it. Voters, educators, and political students must remain vigilant in their consumption of information, recognizing the powerful role that technology plays in influencing the narratives that shape political realities. The ongoing evolution of technology will undoubtedly continue to redefine the landscape of political persuasion, making it essential for stakeholders to adapt and respond to these changes thoughtfully.

Preparing for Future Elections and Campaigns

Preparing for future elections and campaigns requires a strategic approach that combines an understanding of voter behaviour, effective messaging, and the evolving landscape of political communication. As the political environment becomes increasingly dynamic, candidates and their teams must adopt innovative methodologies to connect with their constituents. This preparation involves not only traditional campaign tactics but also an emphasis on narrative crafting, ensuring that the message resonates deeply with voters' values and aspirations.

A critical aspect of preparing for future elections is engaging in comprehensive research to understand the electorate. This includes analysing demographic shifts, voter preferences, and significant issues that impact the community. Campaign teams should conduct surveys, focus groups, and town hall meetings to gather insights into what matters most to voters. By identifying key topics and concerns, candidates can tailor their narratives to address these issues, making them more relatable and compelling to the electorate.

Another important element is the development of a coherent and persuasive campaign narrative. This narrative should be authentic and reflect the candidate's values, experiences, and vision for the future. Crafting a strong story not only helps to differentiate a candidate from their opponents but also fosters emotional connections with voters. Ensuring that the narrative is consistent across various platforms—from social media to public speeches—reinforces the candidate's message and builds trust among the electorate.

In addition to narrative crafting, it is essential for campaigns to utilize modern communication tools effectively. The rise of digital media has transformed how candidates interact with voters, providing opportunities for direct engagement and real-time feedback. Campaigns should leverage social media, email newsletters, and online forums to disseminate their messages and encourage dialogue. By embracing these platforms, candidates can reach a broader audience, especially younger voters who are more inclined to engage with political content online.

Finally, preparing for future elections also involves the cultivation of a dedicated and informed volunteer base. Volunteers play a crucial role in grassroots campaigning, helping to spread the candidate's message and mobilize voters. Training and empowering volunteers with the necessary skills and knowledge can significantly enhance a campaign's reach and effectiveness. By fostering a sense of community and shared purpose among supporters, candidates can create a robust network of advocates who are passionate about driving the campaign forward and ensuring voter turnout on election day.

Examples of winning campaigns

Here are some of the most successful political campaigns from the last 50 years:

1. Barack Obama 2008 Campaign: Barack Obama's 2008 presidential campaign was marked by its innovative use of social media and grassroots organizing, leading to his historic election as the first African American president of the United States.

2. Ronald Reagan 1980 Campaign: Ronald Reagan's 1980 presidential campaign focused on slogans like "Make America Great Again" and his conservative vision for the country, ultimately leading to his victory over incumbent President Jimmy Carter.

3. Margaret Thatcher 1979 Campaign: Margaret Thatcher's 1979 campaign for Prime Minister of the United Kingdom was centered around her strong leadership and promise to revive the country's economy, earning her the nickname "The Iron Lady."

4. Justin Trudeau 2015 Campaign: Justin Trudeau's 2015 campaign for Prime Minister of Canada focused on inclusivity, diversity, and a message of hope and change, leading to his Liberal Party's victory and his appointment as Prime Minister.

5. Angela Merkel 2005 Campaign: Angela Merkel's 2005 campaign for Chancellor of Germany focused on her pragmatic leadership style and commitment to economic reform, ultimately leading to her becoming the first female Chancellor of Germany.

These campaigns were successful for various reasons, including effective messaging, strong leadership qualities, and the ability to resonate with voters on key issues.

Successful campaigning requires a combination of strategic planning, clear messaging, effective communication, and strong execution. A brilliant campaign can connect with its target audience, mobilize support, and inspire action. It involves understanding the needs and concerns of the audience, identifying key issues, setting specific goals, and implementing a variety of tactics to achieve those goals. Additionally, successful campaigns often leverage various channels and platforms, such as social media, traditional media, events, and grassroots organizing, to reach and engage with a wide range of stakeholders. Adapting to changing circumstances, listening to feedback, and being responsive are also important aspects of successful campaigning. Ultimately, a brilliant campaign is one that is able to effectively communicate its message, build momentum, and achieve its objectives

Here is your Campaign checklist

Followed by notes pages

This checklist assumes the candidate has already built up a solid background and is known for their work and abilities so a campaign can be built around them. If not, then start building a brand for any candidate before starting a successful campaign.

A checklist for a political campaign involves several key tasks and considerations.

1. Define Your Campaign Goals: - Establish clear campaign objectives - Identify target audience and voters - Develop key messages and campaign themes

2. Build Your Team: - Recruit campaign mgr, admin staff and volunteers - Assign roles and responsibilities - Establish communication channels

3. Fundraising and Budgeting: - Create a fundraising plan - Set a budget for the campaign - Identify potential donors and fundraising strategies.

4. Develop Your Campaign Strategy: - Develop a campaign timeline and schedule - Create a voter outreach plan - Determine campaign tactics (e.g., advertising, events, canvassing)

5. Get on the Ballot: - Meet all legal requirements to get on the ballot - Submit necessary paperwork and documentation - Ensure compliance with election laws and regulations

6. Voter Outreach and Engagement: - Door-to-door canvassing - Phone banking - Organize meetings and other events - Engage with voters through social media and other platforms

7. Communications and Messaging: - Develop a strong campaign message - Create campaign materials (e.g., flyers, posters, website) - Implement a media strategy

8. Get Endorsements: - Seek endorsements from community leaders, organizations, and influential individuals - Use endorsements in campaign materials and messaging

9. Get Out the Vote (GOTV): - Develop a GOTV plan - Mobilize volunteers to help with voter turnout efforts - Ensure voters have necessary information about polling locations and voting procedures.

10. Monitor and Evaluate: - Track campaign progress and performance - Collect feedback from voters - Adjust the campaign strategy as needed.

Remember that this checklist can be customized based on the specific needs and goals of your political campaign.

Good luck with your campaign!

NOTES

NOTES

NOTES

NOTES

NOTES

NOTES

NOTES

<u>NOTES</u>

NOTES

NOTES

NOTES

NOTES

NOTES

NOTES

NOTES

NOTES

<u>NOTES</u>